ASSESSMENT BOOK

GRADE 3

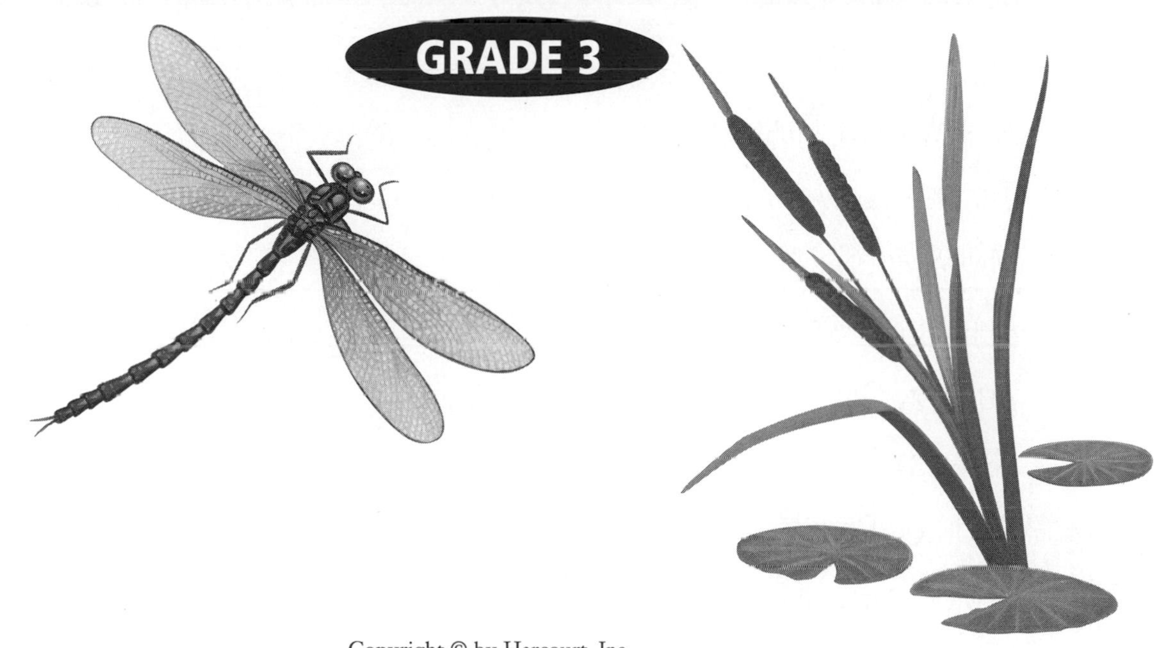

Printed in the United States of America

ISBN 0-15-334585-3

2 3 4 5 6 7 8 9 10 073 10 09 08 07 06 05 04 03 02

Orlando Austin Chicago New York Toronto London San Diego

Visit *The Learning Site!*
www.harcourtschool.com

CONTENTS

Name ______________________________ Pretest

Phonics

Directions: Fill in the circle next to the word that names the picture.

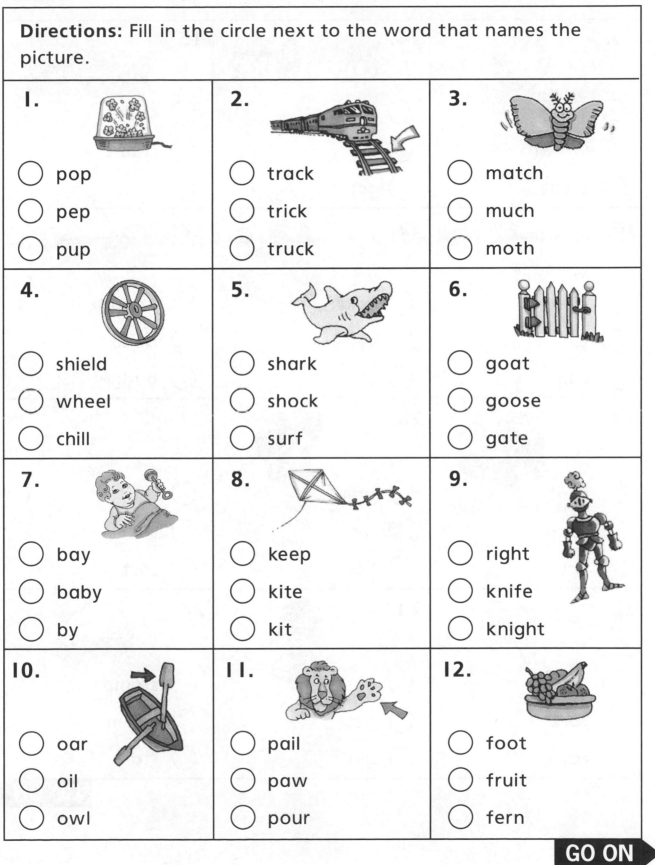

1. ○ pop ○ pep ○ pup	**2.** ○ track ○ trick ○ truck	**3.** ○ match ○ much ○ moth
4. ○ shield ○ wheel ○ chill	**5.** ○ shark ○ shock ○ surf	**6.** ○ goat ○ goose ○ gate
7. ○ bay ○ baby ○ by	**8.** ○ keep ○ kite ○ kit	**9.** ○ right ○ knife ○ knight
10. ○ oar ○ oil ○ owl	**11.** ○ pail ○ paw ○ pour	**12.** ○ foot ○ fruit ○ fern

GO ON

Name ______________________________ Pretest

Phonics (continued)

13. ◯ when ◯ wreath ◯ treat	**14.** ◯ force ◯ fir ◯ fourth	**15.** ◯ shore ◯ shout ◯ stew
16. ◯ cried ◯ cube ◯ cue	**17.** ◯ cold ◯ cycle ◯ child	**18.** ◯ bound ◯ bone ◯ budge
19. ◯ coat ◯ cage ◯ cot	**20.** ◯ bold ◯ by ◯ bow	**21.** ◯ shirt ◯ short ◯ sort
22. ◯ card ◯ cork ◯ cook	**23.** ◯ gas ◯ get ◯ girl	**24.** ◯ stamp ◯ storm ◯ start

GO ON

Phonics (continued)

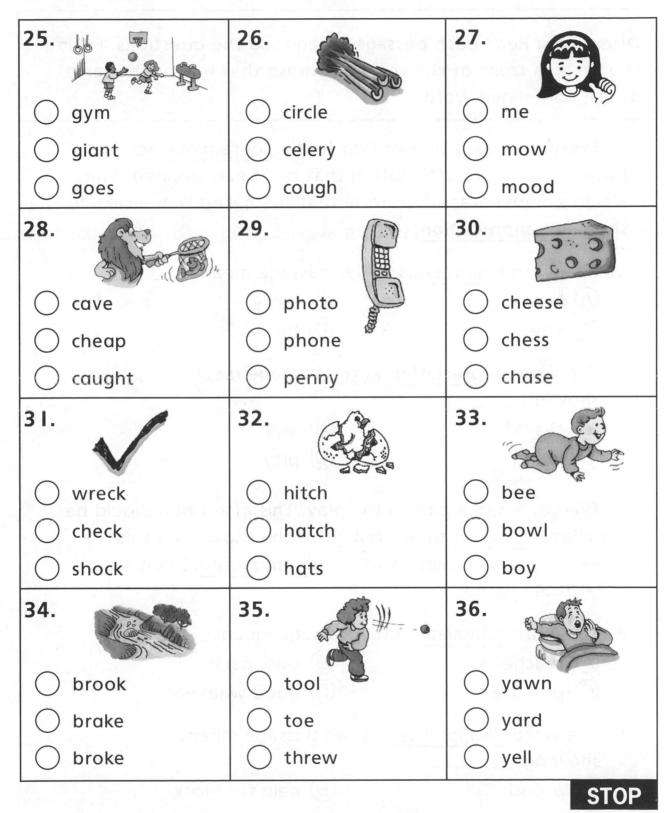

25. ◯ gym ◯ giant ◯ goes	**26.** ◯ circle ◯ celery ◯ cough	**27.** ◯ me ◯ mow ◯ mood
28. ◯ cave ◯ cheap ◯ caught	**29.** ◯ photo ◯ phone ◯ penny	**30.** ◯ cheese ◯ chess ◯ chase
31. ◯ wreck ◯ check ◯ shock	**32.** ◯ hitch ◯ hatch ◯ hats	**33.** ◯ bee ◯ bowl ◯ boy
34. ◯ brook ◯ brake ◯ broke	**35.** ◯ tool ◯ toe ◯ threw	**36.** ◯ yawn ◯ yard ◯ yell

STOP

Name____ Pretest

Vocabulary in Context

Directions: Read each passage. Then read the questions. Fill in the circle in front of the word or phrase that means the same as the underlined word.

Everyone was proud of Dan for his courageous act. He bravely saved the little kitten that had been trapped. The kitten's owner was so grateful that she baked Dan a cake to show her appreciation.

1. The word courageous in this passage means ________.
   - Ⓐ late
   - Ⓑ lucky
   - Ⓒ silly
   - Ⓓ brave

2. The word appreciation in this passage means showing ________.
   - Ⓐ thanks
   - Ⓑ fear
   - Ⓒ humor
   - Ⓓ pity

Everyone had a part in the play. This afternoon would be their last rehearsal to get ready for the show. Dan said, "I hope no one who sees us will be disappointed. I don't want to let them down."

3. The word rehearsal in this passage means ________.
   - Ⓐ teacher
   - Ⓑ class party
   - Ⓒ practice
   - Ⓓ good weather

4. The word disappointed in this passage means showing ________.
   - Ⓐ proud
   - Ⓑ paid for work
   - Ⓒ hungry
   - Ⓓ let down

STOP

Score ________

Directions: Read each passage. Then read the question that follows the passage. Fill in the circle in front of the correct answer for each question.

The airplane is one of the best ways people have of traveling from place to place. A jet airliner can carry people halfway around the world in just hours. By refueling in the air, some planes can fly around the world without stopping. Airplanes can fly even faster than sound.

1. Which of these is an opinion from the passage?
   - Ⓐ Airplanes can fly even faster than sound.
   - Ⓑ By refueling in the air, some planes can fly around the world without stopping.
   - Ⓒ A jet airliner can carry people halfway around the world in just hours.
   - Ⓓ The airplane is one of the best ways people have of traveling from place to place.

2. Which word part makes the word refueling mean "fuel **again**"?
   - Ⓐ fuel
   - Ⓑ re-
   - Ⓒ -ling
   - Ⓓ -ing

GO ON

Comprehension and Skills (continued)

Burt kicked his legs up and down swiftly as he surged through the water. He stroked as hard as he could, forcing his way through the water, while being careful to stay in his lane. He glanced over and saw that he was ahead of the others. Maybe he would win!

3. Based on clues from the passage, which of these is the best definition for **surged**?

Ⓐ moved powerfully
Ⓑ made a mess
Ⓒ played water polo
Ⓓ moved slowly

4. Which of these words from the passage is a synonym for **glanced**?

Ⓐ kicked
Ⓑ careful
Ⓒ looked
Ⓓ stroked

GO ON

Sally was in her room, getting ready to go shopping with Dad.

"Have you finished studying for your test?" Dad asked.

"Yes, Dad. I'm through studying. I'll be right there," Sally answered.

Sally looked over at the open book on her desk. This morning, Dad had told her that he would not take her shopping for a new dress until she had studied to get ready for the big test tomorrow. Because she wanted to go shopping, Sally had rushed through her studies, barely looking at the chapters that would be on the test.

Sally went into the living room where Dad was waiting.

"I'm sorry, Dad," she said. "I don't think you should take me shopping for the dress after all. I really need to study more tonight. I want to make sure I have learned all I need to know to do well on the test."

"I'm glad to hear you say that, Sally. And don't worry—we can always shop for the new dress this weekend."

GO ON

5. Where does this story take place?
   Ⓐ at Sally's house
   Ⓑ in a store
   Ⓒ at school
   Ⓓ in Dad's office

6. What is Sally's problem in the story?
   Ⓐ She has not done a report that is due.
   Ⓑ She needs to earn money to buy a dress.
   Ⓒ She knows she should study before she has fun.
   Ⓓ She needs help with her homework.

7. How does Dad feel when Sally tells him the truth?
   Ⓐ angry
   Ⓑ understanding
   Ⓒ disappointed
   Ⓓ lucky

8. What will Sally probably do next?
   Ⓐ She will stay up late talking to Dad.
   Ⓑ She will study for her test.
   Ⓒ She will go to bed.
   Ⓓ She will go shopping with Dad.

GO ON

Comprehension and Skills (continued)

To teach a dog a trick, the first thing you must do is to get the dog to understand what you want it to do. For example, if you want a dog to stand up, you might lift up its front paws and say "Stand up." When the dog does what you want, you should praise and reward the dog to let it know it has pleased you. You might say "Good dog!" and pet the dog's head or give it something good to eat. After you do this for a while, the dog will do what you say when you give it a command.

Be careful, though, not to spend too much time teaching the dog a trick. Work with the dog only once or twice a day, and do not spend more than about 15 minutes teaching the dog. If you spend too much time, the dog might get tired and lose interest.

GO ON

Comprehension and Skills (continued)

9. What is the first thing to do when you teach a dog a trick?
   - Ⓐ Say kind words.
   - Ⓑ Give the dog something to eat.
   - Ⓒ Pet the dog.
   - Ⓓ Show the dog what you want it to do.

10. You should not spend too much time teaching a dog a trick because it might make the dog ________.
   - Ⓐ try to bite
   - Ⓑ get tired
   - Ⓒ run away
   - Ⓓ become afraid

11. About how long should you work with a dog to teach it a trick?
   - Ⓐ 15 minutes a day
   - Ⓑ 1 day
   - Ⓒ 2 days
   - Ⓓ 15 days

12. What is the best summary of the first paragraph?
   - Ⓐ If you want a dog to stand up, you might lift up its front paws.
   - Ⓑ When the dog does what you want, you should praise and reward the dog.
   - Ⓒ You might say "Good dog," and pet the dog's head.
   - Ⓓ To teach a dog a trick, you must show the dog what you want it to do, then praise or reward the dog, and after a while the dog will do what you say when you give it a command.

STOP

Score ________

Directions: Fill in the circle next to the word that names the picture.

1. ○ pop ○ pot ○ pup	**2.** ○ cat ○ cot ○ hot	**3.** ○ ball ○ bill ○ bad
4. ○ him ○ hit ○ ham	**5.** ○ wag ○ wig ○ wall	**6.** ○ sick ○ sock ○ sack
7. ○ pin ○ fin ○ pan	**8.** ○ map ○ mop ○ mix	**9.** ○ lip ○ lap ○ lit
10. ○ top ○ tap ○ tip	**11.** ○ hot ○ hit ○ hat	**12.** ○ fan ○ fin ○ pin

STOP

Score ________

Directions: Read each sentence. Fill in the circle under the word that best completes each sentence.

1. My sister plays the piano while I ________.

light	apples	dance	enough
Ⓐ	Ⓑ	Ⓒ	Ⓓ

2. I have to finish my ________ before I can play.

walks	magnets	lost	homework
Ⓐ	Ⓑ	Ⓒ	Ⓓ

3. Harry gave his permission slip to his ________.

teacher	attract	would	trees
Ⓐ	Ⓑ	Ⓒ	Ⓓ

4. Dustin and James like to ________ stories together.

eye	pound	write	calls
Ⓐ	Ⓑ	Ⓒ	Ⓓ

5. Many people think that dogs make good ________.

story	pets	nights	smile
Ⓐ	Ⓑ	Ⓒ	Ⓓ

STOP

Score ________

Directions: For items 1–8, fill in the circle in front of the correct answer. For items 9–10, write the answer.

1. Where does this story take place?
   - Ⓐ in a classroom
   - Ⓑ in Pam's bedroom
   - Ⓒ in the schoolyard
   - Ⓓ at Pam's house

2. What does Teacher Dan ask the class to do for homework?
   - Ⓐ bring their pets to school
   - Ⓑ draw a creative picture
   - Ⓒ write a creative story
   - Ⓓ make up a dance

3. Why does Teacher Dan ask the class to read the ad?
   - Ⓐ to see if the class is creative
   - Ⓑ to find out how to visit "Matt's Story Stack"
   - Ⓒ to practice reading ads
   - Ⓓ to learn what they are to do for homework

4. Pam does not have a pet crab any longer because _________.
   - Ⓐ the crab did not make a great pet
   - Ⓑ the crab ran away
   - Ⓒ the crab did not like Pam
   - Ⓓ she wanted a pet she could pat

5. After Teacher Dan asks Pam if she likes pets, he asks if she likes _________.
   - Ⓐ to play
   - Ⓑ flags
   - Ⓒ dogs
   - Ⓓ to sing and dance

GO ON

6. The last question Teacher Dan asks Pam is if she likes ________.
   - Ⓐ to dance
   - Ⓑ pets
   - Ⓒ Matt the Cat
   - Ⓓ tan flags

7. A creative story is a story that is mostly ________.
   - Ⓐ facts
   - Ⓑ about cats
   - Ⓒ make-believe
   - Ⓓ a play

8. Someone who is responsible ________.
   - Ⓐ is very funny
   - Ⓑ is always sad
   - Ⓒ can be trusted
   - Ⓓ is not pretty

9. How does Pam feel about her homework at the beginning of the story? How does she feel at the end of the story?

____

____

____

10. What do you think Matt's Story Stack is?

____

____

____

STOP

Directions: Fill in the circle next to the word that names the picture.

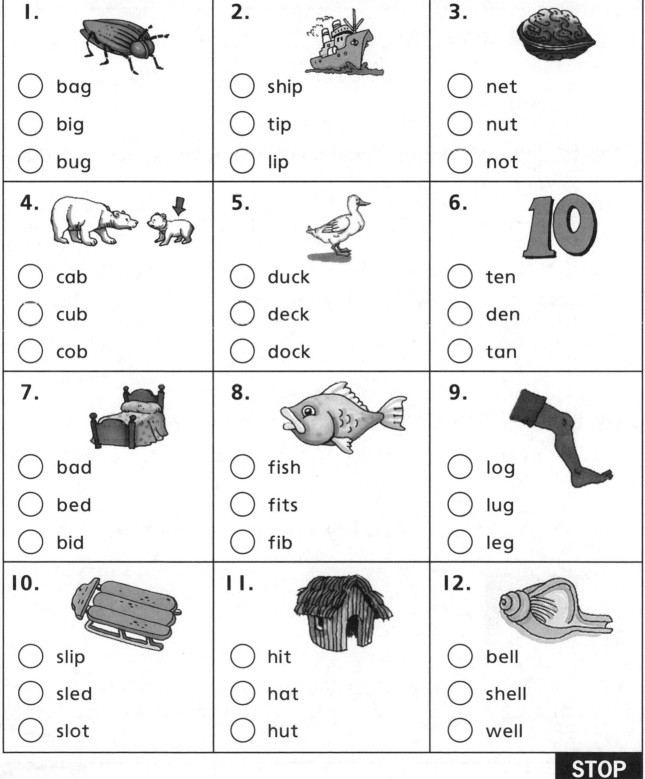

1.	2.	3.
○ bag	○ ship	○ net
○ big	○ tip	○ nut
○ bug	○ lip	○ not

4.	5.	6.
○ cab	○ duck	○ ten
○ cub	○ deck	○ den
○ cob	○ dock	○ tan

7.	8.	9.
○ bad	○ fish	○ log
○ bed	○ fits	○ lug
○ bid	○ fib	○ leg

10.	11.	12.
○ slip	○ hit	○ bell
○ sled	○ hat	○ shell
○ slot	○ hut	○ well

STOP

Directions: Read each sentence. Fill in the circle under the word that best completes each sentence.

1. My mom helped me pack my ________ for our family trip.

suitcase	smelled	early	answers
Ⓐ	Ⓑ	Ⓒ	Ⓓ

2. Sometimes it's more fun to play games with a ________ than by yourself.

creatures	workable	friend	nice
Ⓐ	Ⓑ	Ⓒ	Ⓓ

3. ________ is my favorite season of all.

Rain	Comfort	Something	Summer
Ⓐ	Ⓑ	Ⓒ	Ⓓ

4. Rosa learned to play soccer at ________.

camp	ignore	letters	average
Ⓐ	Ⓑ	Ⓒ	Ⓓ

5. I like it when ________ knows that it's my birthday.

suggested	everyone	bloom	reason
Ⓐ	Ⓑ	Ⓒ	Ⓓ

STOP

Directions: For items 1–8, fill in the circle in front of the correct answer. For items 9–10, write the answer.

1. This story is most like a ________.

   Ⓐ poem Ⓑ play
   Ⓒ letter Ⓓ math book

2. What does Todd tell his mom about the thing in his suitcase?

   Ⓐ It doesn't bite.
   Ⓑ It is poisonous.
   Ⓒ It isn't poisonous.
   Ⓓ There's a spot on it.

3. Todd's sock hops because ________.

   Ⓐ it is a magic sock
   Ⓑ there's a frog in it
   Ⓒ there's a snake in it
   Ⓓ there's a spot on it

4. What happens when Todd puts rocks in his suitcase?

   Ⓐ The suitcase rips.
   Ⓑ He can fix the suitcase.
   Ⓒ The sock hops out.
   Ⓓ The snake likes the rocks.

5. What happens after Todd's suitcase rips?

   Ⓐ He loses his harmonica.
   Ⓑ He finds a frog in his sock.
   Ⓒ He goes home on the bus.
   Ⓓ He finds a hot dog.

GO ON

6. Todd loses his harmonica because ________.

Ⓐ he hits it on the rock
Ⓑ Counselor Bob drops it in the pond
Ⓒ he drops it in his suitcase
Ⓓ he drops it in the pond

7. In this story, Todd's hot dog is ________.

Ⓐ something to eat
Ⓑ a frog
Ⓒ an animal that smells
Ⓓ a suitcase

8. The last letter in this story is different from the others because it is from ________.

Ⓐ Todd to his dad
Ⓑ Todd to his mom
Ⓒ Mom to Dad
Ⓓ Mom to Todd

9. How do you know Counselor Bob does not like Todd's harmonica playing?

____

____

____

10. Everyone cheers when Todd loses his harmonica because

____

____

____

STOP

Directions: Fill in the circle next to the word that names the picture.

1.	2.	3.
○ match ○ much ○ moth	○ shell ○ wheel ○ chill	○ shark ○ shock ○ shuck
4.	**5.**	**6.**
○ pat ○ path ○ patch	○ best ○ chest ○ test	○ branch ○ brand ○ brash
7.	**8.**	**9.**
○ thin ○ shin ○ chin	○ swims ○ switch ○ swish	○ bush ○ bump ○ bunch
10.	**11.**	**12.**
○ star ○ stamp ○ stall	○ cod ○ call ○ card	○ whip ○ sip ○ ship

STOP

Directions: Read each sentence. Fill in the circle under the word that best completes each sentence.

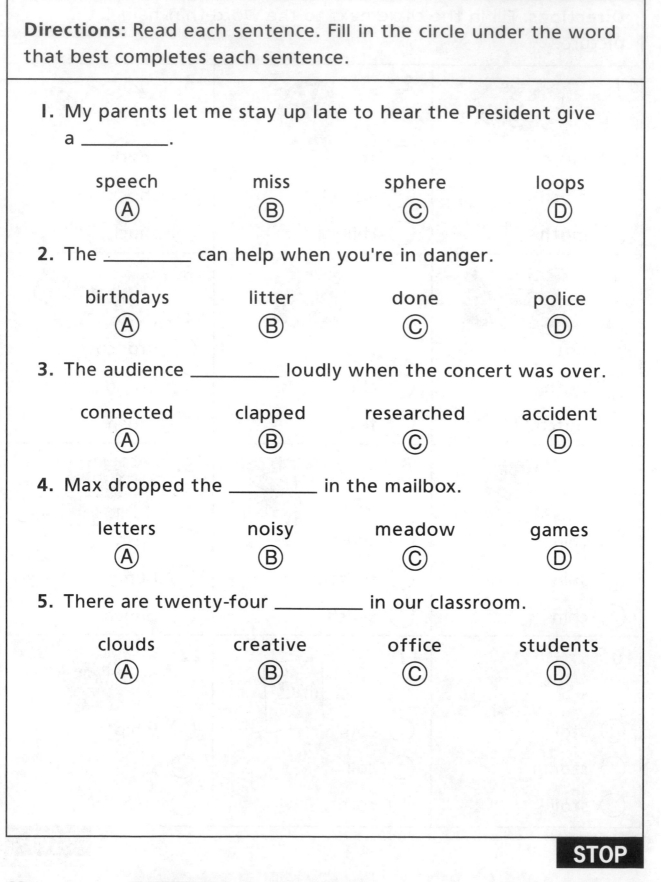

1. My parents let me stay up late to hear the President give a ________.

speech	miss	sphere	loops
Ⓐ	Ⓑ	Ⓒ	Ⓓ

2. The ________ can help when you're in danger.

birthdays	litter	done	police
Ⓐ	Ⓑ	Ⓒ	Ⓓ

3. The audience ________ loudly when the concert was over.

connected	clapped	researched	accident
Ⓐ	Ⓑ	Ⓒ	Ⓓ

4. Max dropped the ________ in the mailbox.

letters	noisy	meadow	games
Ⓐ	Ⓑ	Ⓒ	Ⓓ

5. There are twenty-four ________ in our classroom.

clouds	creative	office	students
Ⓐ	Ⓑ	Ⓒ	Ⓓ

STOP

Score ________

Directions: For items 1–8, fill in the circle in front of the correct answer. For items 9–10, write the answer.

1. In this story, what is Justin's problem?
   - Ⓐ He likes to write letters.
   - Ⓑ He has letters that need to get out.
   - Ⓒ He worries how his letters will get out.
   - Ⓓ Ron Summs

2. The three people that Justin knows can't get out the letters because they ________.
   - Ⓐ are all busy
   - Ⓑ have all had accidents
   - Ⓒ don't want to do it
   - Ⓓ fell in the tub

3. Jessica got the job of getting the letters out because ________.
   - Ⓐ she obeys commands and goes fast
   - Ⓑ she jumps up and down
   - Ⓒ Jessica has fun
   - Ⓓ it is a rush job

4. Jessica is a ________.
   - Ⓐ cat
   - Ⓑ kangaroo
   - Ⓒ dancer
   - Ⓓ jumper

5. In this story, a big grin is a ________.
   - Ⓐ sad face
   - Ⓑ big smile
   - Ⓒ happy face
   - Ⓓ loud cry

GO ON

6. When Justin sees Jessica, she is ________.

Ⓐ jumping up and down
Ⓑ going to dancing school
Ⓒ winning a game
Ⓓ looking for a job

7. Jessica does not make a speech when asked because she ________.

Ⓐ can't talk
Ⓑ hops fast
Ⓒ hugs the kids
Ⓓ goes to Miss Drum's class

8. All the following are characters in this story **except** ________.

Ⓐ Jessica
Ⓑ Pat
Ⓒ Justin
Ⓓ Miss Drum

9. Why do the students in Miss Drum's class beg Jessica to visit them?

____

____

____

10. Why is Jessica able to go fast and get all the letters out?

____

____

____

STOP

Score ________

Name ____________________ Selection Test

Phonics *Creature Clicks*

Directions: Fill in the circle next to the word that names the picture.

1. ○ oar ○ out ○ owl	**2.** ○ corn ○ crop ○ crown	**3.** ○ fur ○ four ○ far
4. ○ mouse ○ miss ○ moss	**5.** ○ fern ○ farm ○ form	**6.** ○ foul ○ far ○ fork
7. ○ gill ○ golf ○ girl	**8.** ○ cloud ○ clod ○ clip	**9.** ○ scar ○ skirt ○ skip
10. ○ tent ○ tarts ○ turtle	**11.** ○ star ○ store ○ stir	**12.** ○ all ○ owl ○ oar

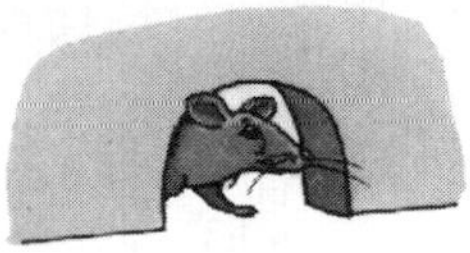

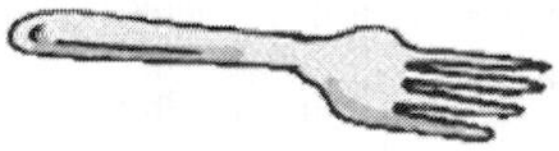

STOP

Score ________

Directions: Read each sentence. Fill in the circle under the word that best completes each sentence.

1. The bird was losing its ________ as it flew.

waters	idea	borrow	feathers
Ⓐ	Ⓑ	Ⓒ	Ⓓ

2. There was only one ________ left on my camera.

far	shot	hairs	place
Ⓐ	Ⓑ	Ⓒ	Ⓓ

3. The farmers watched the chick ________ out of the egg.

hatch	notice	nice	parted
Ⓐ	Ⓑ	Ⓒ	Ⓓ

4. We were able to ________ the movie and have popcorn.

sat	decorated	watch	furrows
Ⓐ	Ⓑ	Ⓒ	Ⓓ

5. Judy's ________ were entered in the art contest!

painted	photos	secret	mouse
Ⓐ	Ⓑ	Ⓒ	Ⓓ

STOP

Directions: For items 1–8, fill in the circle in front of the correct answer. For items 9–10, write the answer.

1. In this story, some adults take pictures of creatures because ________.
   - Ⓐ they like to watch creatures
   - Ⓑ it's their job
   - Ⓒ it's their hobby
   - Ⓓ they want to study creatures

2. All of the creatures listed here can live without sun **except** ________.
   - Ⓐ fish
   - Ⓑ clams
   - Ⓒ crabs
   - Ⓓ people

3. In this story, <u>collapsed</u> means ________.
   - Ⓐ down
   - Ⓑ got up
   - Ⓒ ran fast
   - Ⓓ was not curious

4. In this story, <u>delicate</u> means ________.
   - Ⓐ very strong
   - Ⓑ not very strong
   - Ⓒ big and heavy
   - Ⓓ black and odd

5. In this story, if a creature survives, it ________.
   - Ⓐ lives
   - Ⓑ eats
   - Ⓒ notices others
   - Ⓓ swims

GO ON

6. Some mother bugs stay next to their eggs because they want to ________.

Ⓐ see if they get eaten
Ⓑ keep the dad bug away from the eggs
Ⓒ take photos of the eggs
Ⓓ be sure nothing harms the eggs

7. How do some father bugs care for the eggs?

Ⓐ They park next to them.
Ⓑ They carry them on their backs.
Ⓒ They eat them.
Ⓓ They go off and swim with the eggs.

8. This story is most like a ________.

Ⓐ science book
Ⓑ tall tale
Ⓒ play
Ⓓ poem

9. In this story, why don't birds harm "the smart bug"?

____
____
____

10. Why is "Creature Clicks" a good title for this story?

____
____
____

STOP

Directions: Fill in the circle next to the word that names the picture.

1. ○ gas ○ gown ○ gate	**2.** ○ kitten ○ kite ○ kit	**3.** ○ mile ○ mule ○ male
4. ○ cane ○ cone ○ can	**5.** ○ pine ○ pie ○ pour	**6.** ○ rock ○ rack ○ rake
7. ○ hot ○ his ○ hose	**8.** ○ tie ○ time ○ tar	**9.** ○ bake ○ bike ○ broke
10. ○ flour ○ flame ○ flies	**11.** ○ drapes ○ dress ○ dries	**12.** ○ ban ○ bond ○ bone

STOP

Score ________

Directions: Read each sentence. Fill in the circle under the word that best completes each sentence.

1. There is a new ________ in our class from Mexico.

moving van	sorting	planting	girl
Ⓐ	Ⓑ	Ⓒ	Ⓓ

2. The dog bit Juan because it didn't like to be ________.

teased	wish	worlds	food
Ⓐ	Ⓑ	Ⓒ	Ⓓ

3. We made a ________ on a shooting star.

familiar	glad	dinner	wish
Ⓐ	Ⓑ	Ⓒ	Ⓓ

4. The mobile hung from the ceiling by a ________.

wood	string	would	fed
Ⓐ	Ⓑ	Ⓒ	Ⓓ

5. Peter loves to fly his ________ on windy days.

kite	meters	pushed	people
Ⓐ	Ⓑ	Ⓒ	Ⓓ

STOP

Directions: For items 1–8, fill in the circle in front of the correct answer. For items 9–10, write the answer.

1. At the beginning of the story, what is Howard's problem?
   - Ⓐ He has to write a letter.
   - Ⓑ His best friend is moving away.
   - Ⓒ He is lonely.
   - Ⓓ He is talking with Beth.

2. The first thing Beth asks Howard to do is to ________.
   - Ⓐ fasten the string to her kite
   - Ⓑ get a new best friend
   - Ⓒ help unwind her kite
   - Ⓓ throw Bow Wow a stick

3. The next thing Beth and Howard do is ________.
   - Ⓐ play trading baskets
   - Ⓑ walk Bow Wow
   - Ⓒ go swimming
   - Ⓓ turn cartwheels

4. A moving van is used to ________.
   - Ⓐ take belongings to a new house
   - Ⓑ attach string to a kite
   - Ⓒ take people to another town
   - Ⓓ move animals and pets to the country

5. Beth helps Howard try to find a new best friend by ________.
   - Ⓐ naming girls they both know
   - Ⓑ naming boys they both know
   - Ⓒ telling Howard to move where Rick moved
   - Ⓓ telling Rick not to move

GO ON

6. In this story, teased means ________.
   (A) annoyed someone
   (B) wished for something
   (C) ran away
   (D) joked with a friend

7. What do Beth and Howard do at the end of the story?
   (A) They play chess.
   (B) They play with Bow Wow.
   (C) They fasten string to a kite.
   (D) They play basketball.

8. This story is most like ________.
   (A) fiction
   (B) science
   (C) a tall tale
   (D) a mystery

9. Why does Howard not want Norman or Jack as a new best friend?

____

____

____

10. Why will Beth make a good new best friend for Howard?

____

____

____

STOP

Name ____________________ Selection Test

Phonics *Trainer for a Day*

Directions: Fill in the circle next to the word that names the picture.

1.	2.	3.
◯ frown ◯ fruit ◯ fern	◯ chew ◯ chart ◯ chop	◯ bake ◯ bike ◯ beak

4.	5.	6.
◯ tray ◯ tree ◯ tries	◯ set ◯ seat ◯ suit	◯ rain ◯ ran ◯ run

7.	8.	9.
◯ cloud ◯ clue ◯ clip	◯ tries ◯ tray ◯ true	◯ flute ◯ flip ◯ flat

10.	11.	12.
◯ new ◯ nail ◯ need	◯ left ◯ lays ◯ leaf	◯ ray ◯ rule ◯ ram

STOP

Score ________

Directions: Read each sentence. Fill in the circle under the word that best completes each sentence.

1. A bouquet of flowers can ________ you up on a gloomy day.

cheer	attract	song	add
Ⓐ	Ⓑ	Ⓒ	Ⓓ

2. I have many friends, but my puppy is a ________ one.

connected	ignore	four	special
Ⓐ	Ⓑ	Ⓒ	Ⓓ

3. Being a trapeze artist requires special ________.

telegraph	foods	training	working dog
Ⓐ	Ⓑ	Ⓒ	Ⓓ

4. My brother needs to practice his handwriting ________.

cities	skills	began	low
Ⓐ	Ⓑ	Ⓒ	Ⓓ

5. It is important to be ________ around a newborn baby.

obeys	noisy	cake	gentle
Ⓐ	Ⓑ	Ⓒ	Ⓓ

STOP

 Score ________

Directions: For items 1–8, fill in the circle in front of the correct answer. For items 9–10, write the answer.

1. Who is telling this story?
   - Ⓐ Janet
   - Ⓑ Jake
   - Ⓒ the boy
   - Ⓓ a working dog

2. Jake is the storyteller's ________.
   - Ⓐ sister
   - Ⓑ dog
   - Ⓒ dad
   - Ⓓ sister's dog

3. Someday Jake will be trained to help ________.
   - Ⓐ Janet
   - Ⓑ a blind person
   - Ⓒ kids at camp
   - Ⓓ a deaf person

4. Jake is all the things listed below **except** ________.
   - Ⓐ smart
   - Ⓑ gentle
   - Ⓒ not trainable
   - Ⓓ friendly

5. What does the storyteller think is one of the best rewards for training Jake?
   - Ⓐ taking Jake on a plane ride
   - Ⓑ playing fetch with Jake
   - Ⓒ taking Jake to school for a day
   - Ⓓ going shopping with Jake

GO ON

6. The story says that it is important to tell Jake that he ________.

Ⓐ must stay clam
Ⓑ is doing a good job
Ⓒ should not chase cats
Ⓓ must sit and stay

7. The boy is Jake's special trainer the day that he takes Jake ________.

Ⓐ for a plane ride
Ⓑ on a bus
Ⓒ on the train trip
Ⓓ to school

8. In this story, to approach Jake means to ________.

Ⓐ yell at the dog
Ⓑ pat the dog
Ⓒ walk up to the dog
Ⓓ train the dog

9. How will the family feel when Jake's training is over?

____

____

____

____

10. Name three places the family takes Jake as part of his training.

____

____

____

____

STOP

Directions: Fill in the circle next to the word that names the picture.

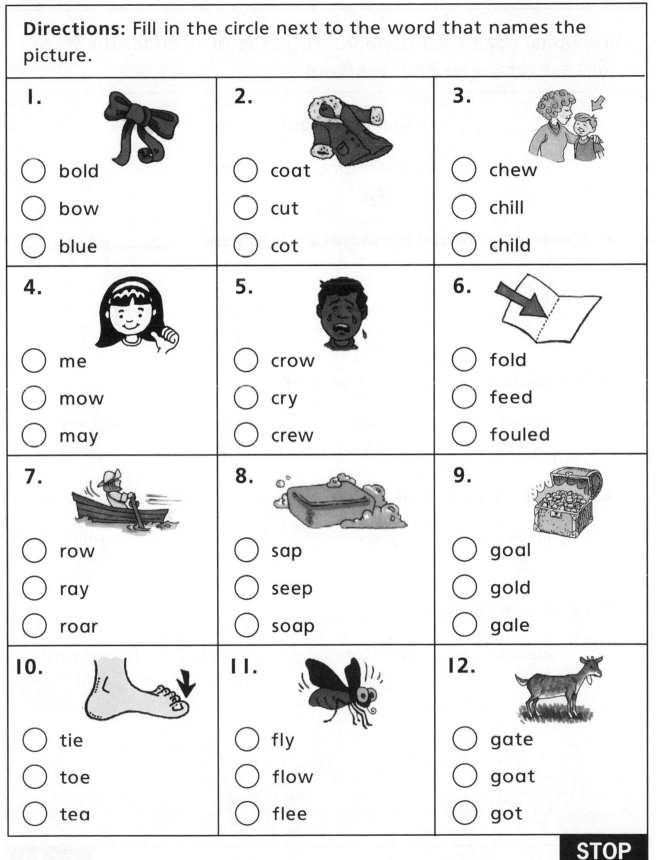

1. ○ bold ○ bow ○ blue	2. ○ coat ○ cut ○ cot	3. ○ chew ○ chill ○ child
4. ○ me ○ mow ○ may	5. ○ crow ○ cry ○ crew	6. ○ fold ○ feed ○ fouled
7. ○ row ○ ray ○ roar	8. ○ sap ○ seep ○ soap	9. ○ goal ○ gold ○ gale
10. ○ tie ○ toe ○ tea	11. ○ fly ○ flow ○ flee	12. ○ gate ○ goat ○ got

STOP

Score ________

Directions: Read each sentence. Fill in the circle under the word that best completes each sentence.

1. The ________ was full and bright.

brunch	temperature	moon	glue
Ⓐ	Ⓑ	Ⓒ	Ⓓ

2. The hunter missed his target and shot the ________ into a tree.

arrow	omelet	mischief	drizzle
Ⓐ	Ⓑ	Ⓒ	Ⓓ

3. The loud ________ made us jump.

done	nose	lake	sound
Ⓐ	Ⓑ	Ⓒ	Ⓓ

4. My dad loves to look at the ________ though his telescope.

summons	stars	hurtful	silly
Ⓐ	Ⓑ	Ⓒ	Ⓓ

5. Most detectives are very ________.

clever	swiftly	pictures	homeward
Ⓐ	Ⓑ	Ⓒ	Ⓓ

STOP

Score ________

Directions: For items 1–8, fill in the circle in front of the correct answer. For items 9–10, write the answer.

1. When does this story take place?
   - Ⓐ yesterday
   - Ⓑ in the present
   - Ⓒ long ago
   - Ⓓ in the future

2. Because the sun, the moon, and the stars were hidden, the world was ________ all the time.
   - Ⓐ dark
   - Ⓑ sunny
   - Ⓒ hot
   - Ⓓ cloudy

3. How are the animals in this story different from the animals of today?
   - Ⓐ Animals of today live in people's homes.
   - Ⓑ Animals in the story could sing, tell stories, and play tricks.
   - Ⓒ Animals of today are more clever.
   - Ⓓ Animals in the story liked living in the dark.

4. In this story, Raven is a ________ bird.
   - Ⓐ dumb
   - Ⓑ fast
   - Ⓒ tired
   - Ⓓ skillful

5. In this story, as swiftly as an arrow over land means Raven ________.
   - Ⓐ could fly very fast
   - Ⓑ had a plan
   - Ⓒ could see for miles
   - Ⓓ was tired of the dark

GO ON

6. Why does Raven not eat the food that the wife gives it?

Ⓐ Raven isn't hungry.
Ⓑ Raven wants playthings.
Ⓒ Raven says, "Gah! Gah! Gah!"
Ⓓ Raven is a pest.

7. When the man lets Raven have the last bag, Raven ________.

Ⓐ gets the moon
Ⓑ gets the stars
Ⓒ lets out the sun
Ⓓ eats all the food

8. In this story, the word clever means ________.

Ⓐ smart
Ⓑ tired
Ⓒ friendly
Ⓓ noisy

9. What event in nature does this story try to explain?

____

____

____

____

10. How is Earth different after Raven opens the three bags?

____

____

____

____

STOP

Name ______________________________ Selection Test

Phonics *This is My Story*

Directions: Fill in the circle next to the word that names the picture.

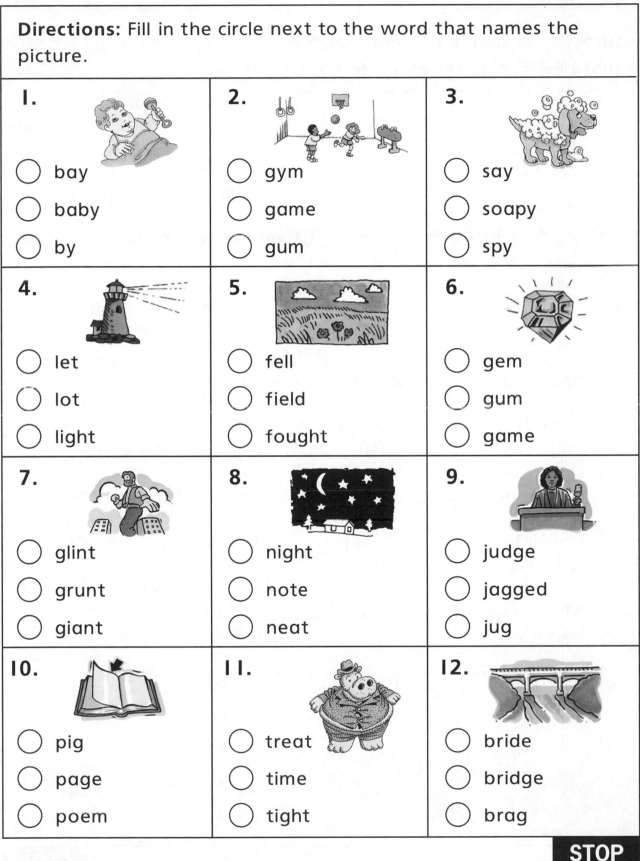

1.

○ bay
○ baby
○ by

2.

○ gym
○ game
○ gum

3.

○ say
○ soapy
○ spy

4.

○ let
○ lot
○ light

5.

○ fell
○ field
○ fought

6.

○ gem
○ gum
○ game

7.

○ glint
○ grunt
○ giant

8.

○ night
○ note
○ neat

9.

○ judge
○ jagged
○ jug

10.

○ pig
○ page
○ poem

11.

○ treat
○ time
○ tight

12.

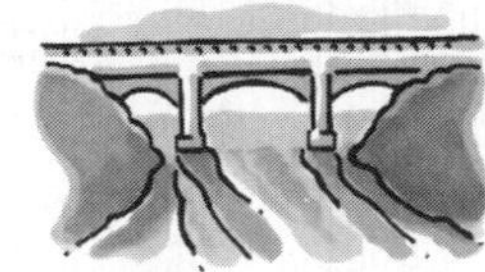

○ bride
○ bridge
○ brag

STOP

Score ________

Directions: Read each sentence. Fill in the circle under the word that best completes each sentence.

1. The librarian helped me find books by my favorite ________.

stone	nonsense	author	ideas
Ⓐ	Ⓑ	Ⓒ	Ⓓ

2. We looked for the ________ of one of the books in the card catalogue.

edges	title	saved	sphere
Ⓐ	Ⓑ	Ⓒ	Ⓓ

3. We ________ the call number down on a card.

advice	depend	equipment	wrote
Ⓐ	Ⓑ	Ⓒ	Ⓓ

4. I explained that ________ are my favorite stories to read.

folktales	bake	evenly	school
Ⓐ	Ⓑ	Ⓒ	Ⓓ

5. My teacher gives us time to ________ our work before we hand it in.

gym	revise	chew	yellow
Ⓐ	Ⓑ	Ⓒ	Ⓓ

STOP

Score ________

Name ______________________________ Selection Test

End-of-Selection Test *This is My Story*

Directions: For items 1–8, fill in the circle in front of the correct answer. For items 9–10, write the answer.

1. This story is mostly about ________.
   - Ⓐ the author as a little girl
   - Ⓑ the author as a writer of children's books
   - Ⓒ the author's first children's book
   - Ⓓ how she wrote the story about a totem pole

2. The person who writes a story is called the ________.
   - Ⓐ artist
   - Ⓑ name
   - Ⓒ author
   - Ⓓ editor

3. The title of a story is the ________ of the story.
   - Ⓐ author
   - Ⓑ artist
   - Ⓒ editor
   - Ⓓ name

4. The title of the first book Diane Hoyt-Goldsmith wrote is ________.
   - Ⓐ *Totem Pole*
   - Ⓑ *Mr. Migdale*
   - Ⓒ *Tales Old and New*
   - Ⓓ *Faraway Lands*

5. What rule about writing stories has the author made for herself?
   - Ⓐ She will write only folktales of long ago.
   - Ⓑ She will write about real children and things.
   - Ⓒ She will write about make-believe children and things.
   - Ⓓ She will draw all the pictures for the books she writes.

GO ON

6. When the author revises a story, she ________.
   (A) is finished with her story
   (B) draws pictures for it
   (C) fixes spelling mistakes
   (D) makes the story sound better

7. If the author begins looking for something to write a new book about, she ________.
   (A) stays home
   (B) travels to a new place
   (C) goes to the library
   (D) visits old friends

8. When the author writes a book, she ________.
   (A) tells the story on a tape recorder
   (B) uses a computer
   (C) writes it by hand first
   (D) never has to revise it

9. What did the author do when she visited David and his family?

____

____

____

10. How does the author compare what she did as a child to what she is doing now?

____

____

____

STOP

Directions: Fill in the circle next to the word that names the picture.

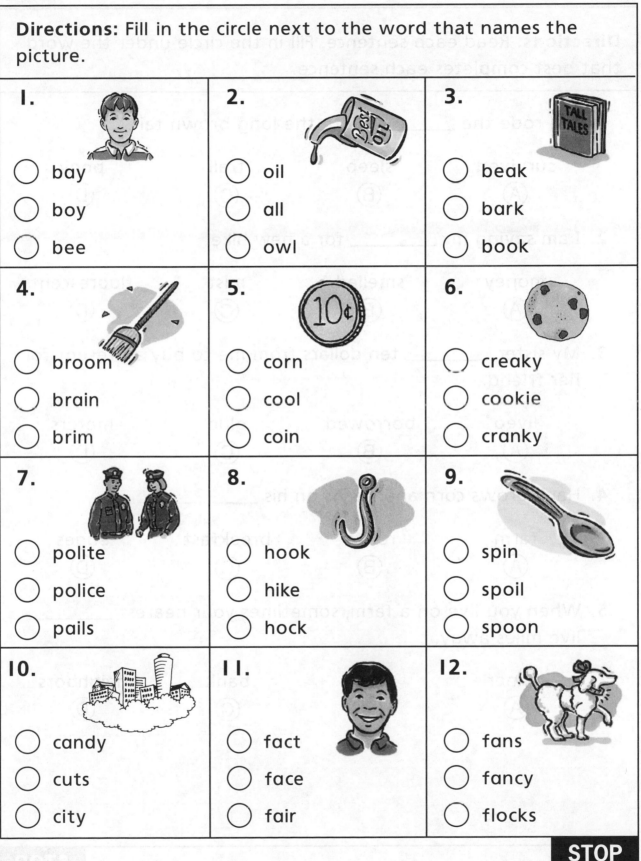

1.	2.	3.
◯ bay ◯ boy ◯ bee	◯ oil ◯ all ◯ owl	◯ beak ◯ bark ◯ book
4.	**5.**	**6.**
◯ broom ◯ brain ◯ brim	◯ corn ◯ cool ◯ coin	◯ creaky ◯ cookie ◯ cranky
7.	**8.**	**9.**
◯ polite ◯ police ◯ pails	◯ hook ◯ hike ◯ hock	◯ spin ◯ spoil ◯ spoon
10.	**11.**	**12.**
◯ candy ◯ cuts ◯ city	◯ fact ◯ face ◯ fair	◯ fans ◯ fancy ◯ flocks

STOP

Directions: Read each sentence. Fill in the circle under the word that best completes each sentence.

1. Ted rode the ________ with the long brown tail.

survived	sleep	trail	pony
Ⓐ	Ⓑ	Ⓒ	Ⓓ

2. I am saving my ________ for a new bike.

money	smelled	mist	fluorescent
Ⓐ	Ⓑ	Ⓒ	Ⓓ

3. My sister ________ ten dollars from me to buy a present for her friend.

lived	borrowed	glue	meters
Ⓐ	Ⓑ	Ⓒ	Ⓓ

4. Hank grows corn and beans on his ________.

farm	recite	breakfast	edges
Ⓐ	Ⓑ	Ⓒ	Ⓓ

5. When you live on a farm, sometimes your nearest ________ live miles away.

dinner	lava	bank	neighbors
Ⓐ	Ⓑ	Ⓒ	Ⓓ

STOP

Directions: For items 1–8, fill in the circle in front of the correct answer. For items 9–10, write the answer.

1. Tyrone wants to know how much money he has in the bank because he wants to know if he ________.
   Ⓐ has enough money to buy a wild pony
   Ⓑ has enough money to buy a horse
   Ⓒ is very rich
   Ⓓ can buy a new saddle for his old pony

2. Ty does all the following jobs for Mrs. Wyman **except** ________.
   Ⓐ sweep the floor
   Ⓑ stack the shelves
   Ⓒ help customers
   Ⓓ clean the back room

3. All the following tell about Blue Sky **except** ________.
   Ⓐ her eyes had a wild look
   Ⓑ her eyes looked sad
   Ⓒ she was friendly
   Ⓓ her coat was very black

4. Ty wants his neighbors to be satisfied with his work, so he ________.
   Ⓐ tries his best
   Ⓑ works very slowly
   Ⓒ eats lunch with Mrs. Bly
   Ⓓ cuts everyone's grass

5. What do the neighbors think Ty is planning to do with the money he earns?
   Ⓐ put it in the bank
   Ⓑ buy a wild horse
   Ⓒ buy feed for the pony
   Ⓓ buy a wild pony

GO ON

6. At an auction, people ________ on what they want to buy.
   Ⓐ sit
   Ⓑ stand
   Ⓒ put
   Ⓓ bid

7. What is Ty afraid will happen at the auction?
   Ⓐ Someone else will buy the pony.
   Ⓑ He won't have enough money for the pony.
   Ⓒ His family won't let him keep the pony.
   Ⓓ The pony will run away.

8. He'll have his hands full if he tries to tame a wild pony in this story means ________.
   Ⓐ the pony will be bigger than both Ty's hands
   Ⓑ it won't be much work to tame the pony
   Ⓒ Ty will find it difficult to train the pony
   Ⓓ Ty won't be able to train that wild pony

9. Do you think Ty planned from the beginning to set Blue Sky free? Why?

____

____

____

10. Why does no one but Ty bid on the pony?

____

____

____

STOP

Directions: Fill in the circle next to the word that names the picture.

1.	2.	3.
○ right ○ sight ○ knight	○ pail ○ paw ○ pour	○ tone ○ stone ○ phone

4.	5.	6.
○ cart ○ caught ○ coat	○ wrist ○ twist ○ mist	○ yawn ○ yard ○ yell

7.	8.	9.
○ land ○ laugh ○ laws	○ gopher ○ goat ○ golf	○ bee ○ see ○ knee

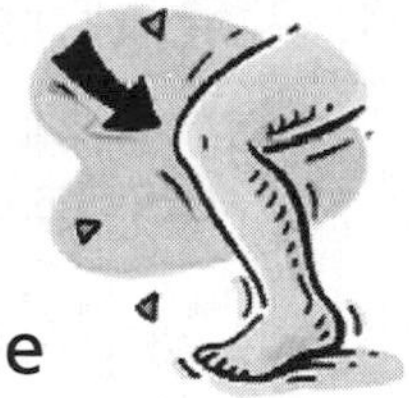

10.	11.	12.
○ hike ○ hawk ○ hook	○ haul ○ hole ○ hail	○ rent ○ wren ○ when

STOP

Score ________

Directions: Read each sentence. Fill in the circle under the word that best completes each sentence.

1. It's fun to skate on the ________ in winter.

eye	ago	ice	trail
Ⓐ	Ⓑ	Ⓒ	Ⓓ

2. Ice is the ________ form of water.

thanked	worlds	office	solid
Ⓐ	Ⓑ	Ⓒ	Ⓓ

3. Our family took our boat to the ________.

island	along	mixed	far
Ⓐ	Ⓑ	Ⓒ	Ⓓ

4. The current in the ________ carried our boat along.

erupting	confident	river	audience
Ⓐ	Ⓑ	Ⓒ	Ⓓ

5. We moved our boat to the side so that the big ________ could pass.

ship	winter	cut	rain
Ⓐ	Ⓑ	Ⓒ	Ⓓ

STOP

Directions: For items 1–8, fill in the circle in front of the correct answer. For items 9–10, write the answer.

1. Who is telling this story?
   - Ⓐ Dad
   - Ⓑ Mom
   - Ⓒ Lizzie
   - Ⓓ Grandpa Jakoby

2. Harvest time is special because ________.
   - Ⓐ there is a party every year
   - Ⓑ during many winters, the bananas freeze
   - Ⓒ a tropical storm may blow away the flowers
   - Ⓓ the family makes memory-makers

3. In this story, a schooner is a ________.
   - Ⓐ special banana
   - Ⓑ memory-maker
   - Ⓒ sailing ship
   - Ⓓ lid on a jar

4. After Lizzie glued the little ship to the jar lid, she ________.
   - Ⓐ put the lid on the jar
   - Ⓑ taped the lid to the jar
   - Ⓒ added water and glitter
   - Ⓓ went to the trading market

5. Lizzie compares ripe bananas to ________.
   - Ⓐ a green frog
   - Ⓑ a yellow school bus
   - Ⓒ her yellow bike
   - Ⓓ leaves reaching the sky

GO ON

6. Lizzie, her dad, and her mom are thankful to Grandma and Grandpa Jakoby for all the following **except** ________.

Ⓐ learning English

Ⓑ planting banana trees

Ⓒ coming to a cold, sunny place

Ⓓ coming to America

7. While the banana bunches are in the tree, they are heavy and ________.

Ⓐ Dad is able to cut the bunch by himself

Ⓑ Mom and Lizzie help support the bunch for Dad

Ⓒ Dad uses a machete to cut down the bananas

Ⓓ there are lots of bananas

8. In this story, the family lives ________.

Ⓐ on an island

Ⓑ by the river

Ⓒ on a large ship

Ⓓ on a banana ranch

9. Name two treats the family makes with bananas.

____

____

____

10. What does the family do with the banana muffins?

____

____

____

STOP

Directions: Fill in the circle next to the word that names the picture.

1. ○ hem ○ ham ○ hum	2. ○ mop ○ map ○ mix	3. ○ well ○ chill ○ shell
4. ○ duck ○ deck ○ dock	5. ○ bugle ○ branch ○ brash	6. ○ which ○ sweets ○ switch
7. ○ cord ○ chart ○ card	8. ○ clouds ○ clowns ○ clones	9. ○ skirt ○ stars ○ score
10. ○ fur ○ four ○ fame	11. ○ tune ○ tie ○ time	12. ○ broke ○ brown ○ bike

STOP

Directions: Read each sentence. Fill in the circle under the word that best completes each sentence.

1. My true friends like me best when I am ________.

tonight	magnets	talks	myself
Ⓐ	Ⓑ	Ⓒ	Ⓓ

2. What is the ________ of your favorite holiday?

date	gym	splinters	mayor
Ⓐ	Ⓑ	Ⓒ	Ⓓ

3. My grandmother and I laugh when we ________ the first time I rode a bike.

ago	cartwheel	charge	remember
Ⓐ	Ⓑ	Ⓒ	Ⓓ

4. The ________ shone brightly in the sky.

rainbow	delicate	expect	school
Ⓐ	Ⓑ	Ⓒ	Ⓓ

5. The kitten whined when Wendy went to school because it was ________.

coldly	ignore	expression	lonely
Ⓐ	Ⓑ	Ⓒ	Ⓓ

STOP

Directions: For items 1–8, fill in the circle in front of the correct answer. For items 9–10, write the answer.

1. This story is mostly about ________.
   - Ⓐ letters written to a friend
   - Ⓑ letters written to a big sister
   - Ⓒ how to care for a garden
   - Ⓓ how to plant a garden

2. This story takes place in the ________.
   - Ⓐ fall
   - Ⓑ winter
   - Ⓒ spring
   - Ⓓ summer

3. On each letter that the girl writes, she puts ________.
   - Ⓐ the date
   - Ⓑ the time
   - Ⓒ a rainbow
   - Ⓓ a flower

4. When the girl worked with her mother in the garden, her mother put her in charge of ________.
   - Ⓐ weeding the sweet peas
   - Ⓑ the flower box
   - Ⓒ picking apples
   - Ⓓ planting the carrot seeds

5. She remembers how her sister helped her make ________.
   - Ⓐ an apple pie
   - Ⓑ a rock garden
   - Ⓒ a secret book
   - Ⓓ carrot soup

GO ON

6. After the girl and her father collect some rocks, they see ________.

Ⓐ more beautiful rocks
Ⓑ some baby foxes
Ⓒ their friend the big fox
Ⓓ tracks in the sand

7. Since the fox is back, the girl thinks it means that ________.

Ⓐ summer is coming
Ⓑ spring is really here
Ⓒ she is a real cook
Ⓓ her sister is not missing much

8. In this story, the sky could not stop crying means ________.

Ⓐ the sky is very sad
Ⓑ it rained and rained
Ⓒ the flower box flooded
Ⓓ there was a beautiful rainbow

9. Why does the girl want to keep a book of days?

____

____

____

10. In this story, what does the girl think is the best news?

____

____

____

STOP

Directions: Fill in the circle next to the word that names the picture.

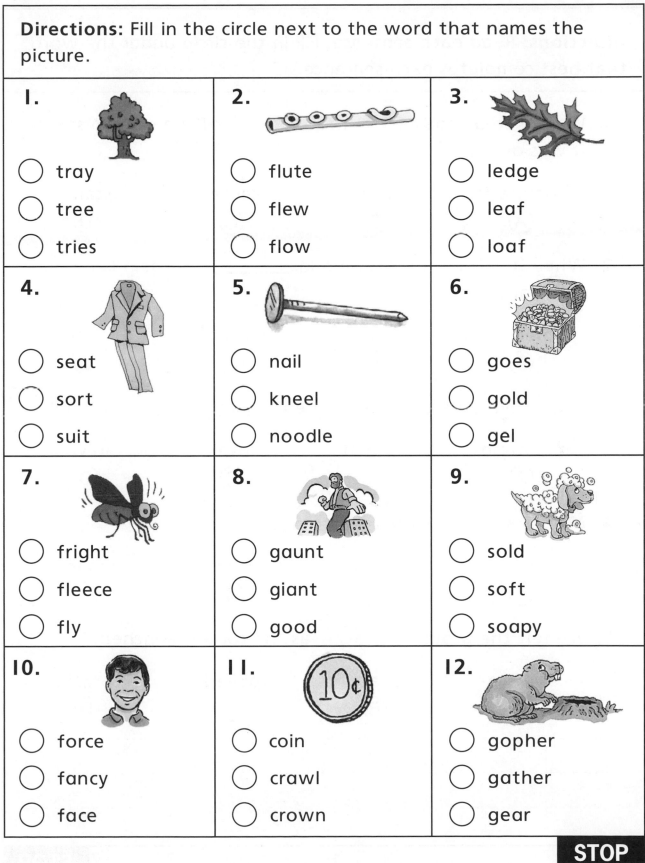

1. ○ tray ○ tree ○ tries	**2.** ○ flute ○ flew ○ flow	**3.** ○ ledge ○ leaf ○ loaf
4. ○ seat ○ sort ○ suit	**5.** ○ nail ○ kneel ○ noodle	**6.** ○ goes ○ gold ○ gel
7. ○ fright ○ fleece ○ fly	**8.** ○ gaunt ○ giant ○ good	**9.** ○ sold ○ soft ○ soapy
10. ○ force ○ fancy ○ face	**11.** ○ coin ○ crawl ○ crown	**12.** ○ gopher ○ gather ○ gear

STOP

Directions: Read each sentence. Fill in the circle under the word that best completes each sentence.

1. We poked a toothpick in the ________ of the cake to see if it was done.

painted	recite	center	stand
Ⓐ	Ⓑ	Ⓒ	Ⓓ

2. When it is cold out, dressing in ________ will help keep you warm.

medals	layers	squirrel	wits
Ⓐ	Ⓑ	Ⓒ	Ⓓ

3. Since I live on a plain, there aren't many ________ to climb.

mountains	present	loves	farewell
Ⓐ	Ⓑ	Ⓒ	Ⓓ

4. Mars is known as the red ________.

crayons	worlds	round	planet
Ⓐ	Ⓑ	Ⓒ	Ⓓ

5. We felt the ground ________ as the rocket launched.

surface	shake	pulled	workable
Ⓐ	Ⓑ	Ⓒ	Ⓓ

STOP

Directions: For items 1–8, fill in the circle in front of the correct answer. For items 9–10, write the answer.

1. Where is the Cascade Range?
   - Ⓐ on the East Coast of North America
   - Ⓑ on the West Coast of South America
   - Ⓒ on the West Coast of North America
   - Ⓓ on the East Coast of South America

2. Long ago this mountain range was formed by ________.
   - Ⓐ melted rocks
   - Ⓑ ice storms
   - Ⓒ rivers
   - Ⓓ volcanoes

3. Hot melted rock is called ________.
   - Ⓐ magma
   - Ⓑ volcano
   - Ⓒ float plates
   - Ⓓ the bulge

4. What happened on Sunday, May 18, 1980?
   - Ⓐ Loggers cut down trees.
   - Ⓑ Mount St. Helens erupted.
   - Ⓒ Ice melted.
   - Ⓓ The sun shone in the afternoon

5. All of the following happened in Yakima, Washington, on May 18, 1980, **except** ________.
   - Ⓐ lightning flashed
   - Ⓑ it snowed
   - Ⓒ it was hard to breathe
   - Ⓓ ash fell from the sky

GO ON

6. The edges of ash were ________.

Ⓐ soft and black
Ⓑ round and heavy
Ⓒ sharp as glass
Ⓓ tiny and black

7. In the center of the crater, ________.

Ⓐ another dome of magma is growing
Ⓑ all is quiet
Ⓒ sometimes lava gushes out
Ⓓ the rivers are clean

8. In this story, shake means ________.

Ⓐ a drink made with milk
Ⓑ to move back and forth
Ⓒ a fancy dance
Ⓓ to upset

9. What did Mount St. Helens look like after it blew?

____

____

____

10. What have we learned about our planet from the Mount St. Helens eruption?

____

____

____

STOP

Name ______________________________ Posttest

Phonics

Directions: Fill in the circle next to the word that names the picture.

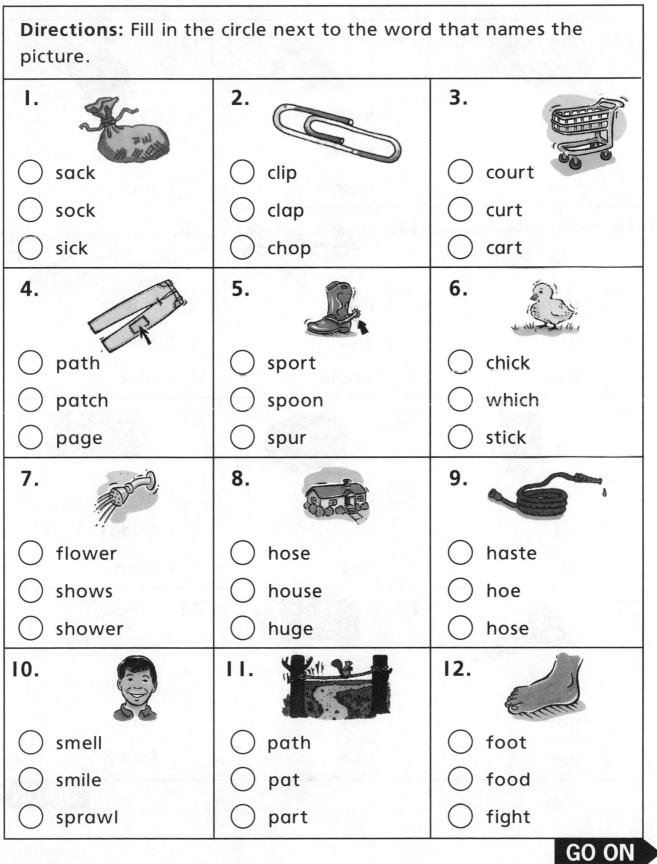

1. ○ sack ○ sock ○ sick	**2.** ○ clip ○ clap ○ chop	**3.** ○ court ○ curt ○ cart
4. ○ path ○ patch ○ page	**5.** ○ sport ○ spoon ○ spur	**6.** ○ chick ○ which ○ stick
7. ○ flower ○ shows ○ shower	**8.** ○ hose ○ house ○ huge	**9.** ○ haste ○ hoe ○ hose
10. ○ smell ○ smile ○ sprawl	**11.** ○ path ○ pat ○ part	**12.** ○ foot ○ food ○ fight

GO ON

Name ______________________________

Phonics (continued)

13.	14.	15.
○ pig ○ page ○ poem	○ beak ○ book ○ bush	○ toy ○ top ○ tap
16.	**17.**	**18.**
○ fresh ○ fish ○ fifth	○ pale ○ wild ○ whale	○ find ○ fold ○ fork
19.	**20.**	**21.**
○ oil ○ owl ○ eel	○ pie ○ pry ○ pea	○ bride ○ bridge ○ brag
22.	**23.**	**24.**
○ roar ○ raise ○ rose	○ tree ○ tray ○ true	○ funnies ○ fudge ○ fancy

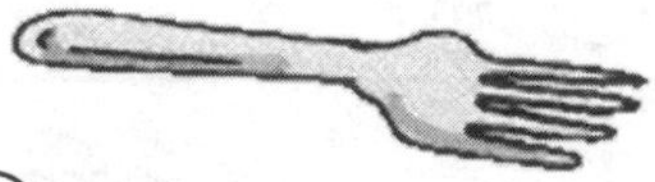

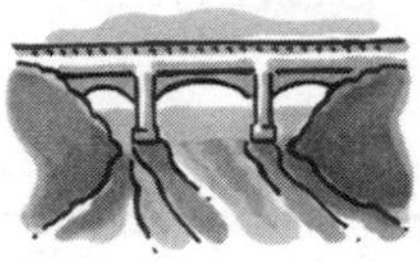

GO ON

Phonics (continued)

25. ○ brook ○ broom ○ bore	**26.** ○ city ○ pity ○ circus	**27.** ○ laps ○ ledge ○ laugh
28. ○ tree ○ knee ○ she	**29.** ○ core ○ court ○ caught	**30.** ○ goat ○ giant ○ gopher
31. ○ wrist ○ we ○ twist	**32.** ○ polite ○ police ○ pour	**33.** ○ cage ○ catch ○ came
34. ○ soil ○ sail ○ sell	**35.** ○ shirts ○ church ○ churns	**36.** ○ flew ○ flute ○ fruit

STOP

Score ________

Name ______________________________ Posttest

Vocabulary in Context

Directions: Read each passage. Then read the questions. Fill in the circle in front of the word or phrase that means the same as the underlined word.

Keri saw Ken's alarmed look. Ken quickly changed his fear into action. After hours of exhausting work, Ken and Keri were tired but happy. They had saved their horses from a nearby fire.

1. The word alarmed in this passage means ________.
   - Ⓐ angry
   - Ⓑ hopeful
   - Ⓒ frightened
   - Ⓓ questioning

2. The word exhausting in this passage means ________.
   - Ⓐ patient
   - Ⓑ very tiring
   - Ⓒ playful
   - Ⓓ puzzling

Leon took a deep breath and inhaled the smells of the garden. All around him there were beautiful colors—red, yellow, lavender, and blue. The garden looked like a rainbow.

3. The word inhaled in this passage means ________.
   - Ⓐ looked at
   - Ⓑ tasted
   - Ⓒ breathed in
   - Ⓓ talked to

4. The word lavender in this passage means ________.
   - Ⓐ dried leaves
   - Ⓑ the color purple
   - Ⓒ a sweet smell
   - Ⓓ a kind of plant

STOP

Score ________

Directions: Read each passage. Fill in the circle in front of the correct answer for each question.

Every spring, seals go to their breeding grounds, called *rookeries*, to have their young. Most rookeries are on islands. Rookeries for northern fur seals are large beach areas. More than 150,000 seals may gather at one rookery. The northern fur seal *bulls* (males) are the first to arrive at the rookeries. The *cows* (females) come in early July. Soon after a cow arrives on shore, she gives birth to a baby seal.

1. What is the main idea of this passage?
   - Ⓐ Most rookeries are on islands.
   - Ⓑ More than 150,000 seals may gather at one rookery.
   - Ⓒ The *cows* (females) come in early July.
   - Ⓓ Every spring, seals go to their breeding grounds, called *rookeries*, to have their young.

2. Which type of seals are the first to arrive at the rookeries?
   - Ⓐ young
   - Ⓑ bulls
   - Ⓒ cows
   - Ⓓ large

GO ON

When Jim got to school, he remembered that he had left his group's report on the kitchen table at home. Today was the last day to turn in the report. All four members of his group would get a bad grade if the report was late. Then Jim remembered that his mom was going to be home all morning. He walked up to the teacher's desk. After talking to the teacher, Jim left the room.

3. Where is Jim when he remembers he left his report?

Ⓐ at lunch

Ⓑ at home

Ⓒ on the bus

Ⓓ at school

4. What will happen when Jim gets back to class?

Ⓐ His mom will bring the report to him later.

Ⓑ He will ask to work with a different group.

Ⓒ He will begin work on a different topic.

Ⓓ He will tell the teacher his group did not do its report.

GO ON

The alligator and the crocodile are alike and different in many ways. It is easy to tell the difference between an American alligator and an American crocodile because the alligator has a much broader snout (muzzle or nose). Alligators are also less fierce and less active than crocodiles. Further, when crocodiles close their jaws, the fourth tooth in each side of their lower jaw sticks out on the outside of the snout. When alligators close their jaws, though, the fourth tooth stays inside and goes into a little pocket in the upper jaw so that you don't see the tooth.

Both alligators and crocodiles are reptiles. They both look like ugly lizards with thick bodies and powerful tails. They both use their strong, short legs to walk on land, but they keep their legs back against the sides of their bodies when they swim.

GO ON

5. Which word part makes the word broader mean "**more broad**"?
   Ⓐ -er
   Ⓑ broad-
   Ⓒ -der
   Ⓓ bro-

6. Which of these words from the passage is a **synonym** for snout?
   Ⓐ jaw
   Ⓑ tooth
   Ⓒ tail
   Ⓓ muzzle

7. When a crocodile closes its jaws, the fourth tooth ________.
   Ⓐ falls out of the jaw
   Ⓑ shows on the outside
   Ⓒ goes up into a pocket
   Ⓓ moves back and forth

8. Which of these is an **opinion** from the passage?
   Ⓐ Both alligators and crocodiles are reptiles.
   Ⓑ They both look like ugly lizards.
   Ⓒ They both use their legs to walk on land.
   Ⓓ They keep their legs back when they swim.

GO ON

Fran was about to meet her pen pal Ingrid, who lives in Germany. For a year now, the two girls had been writing letters to each other. They had traded pictures of themselves, but they had never met before. Now, Ingrid and her family were coming to America for a vacation trip, and they were going to be in San Antonio, Texas, where Fran lives. Fran and her mom were on the way to meet Ingrid at the airport.

"What if we don't like each other?" Fran worried aloud.

"I'm sure you'll get along fine. After all, you have learned a lot about each other already through your letters," Mom told her.

Soon, Fran and her mom were waiting at the gate, looking for a familiar face among all the passengers.

"There she is!" Fran yelled. "That's got to be Ingrid!"

A young girl came running over to Fran. She gave Fran a big hug and said, in very good English, "Fran! You look just like your picture! I am so happy to meet you!"

"We are going to have a really good time!" Fran said.

GO ON

Comprehension and Skills (continued)

9. How does Fran feel as she goes to meet her pen pal?

Ⓐ angry
Ⓑ annoyed
Ⓒ worried
Ⓓ bored

10. What causes Ingrid to come to America?

Ⓐ She is moving to San Antonio, Texas.
Ⓑ She wants to learn English.
Ⓒ She is taking a vacation with her family.
Ⓓ She has run out of letters.

11. Based on clues from the passage, which of these is the best definition of **passengers**?

Ⓐ travelers
Ⓑ letters from foreign countries
Ⓒ friends
Ⓓ confused and foolish

12. What is the best summary for the last two paragraphs?

Ⓐ Fran and Ingrid will be glad when their visit is over.
Ⓑ Fran and Ingrid will enjoy their time together.
Ⓒ Fran and Ingrid will be sorry they finally met.
Ⓓ Fran and Ingrid will stop writing to each other.

STOP

Score ________